The Clairvoyant Practitioner

A Simple Guide to Developing
Your Clairvoyant Abilities

by

Tori Quisling

Upaya House Publishing

Cover design by Austin Williams & Erik Quisling
Layout by Erik Quisling

Library of Congress Cataloging-in-publication Data

07 06 05 04 03   5 4 3 2 1
First Edition

Quisling, Tori
        The Clairvoyant Practitioner: A Simple Guide to Developing Your Clairvoyant Abilities / Tori Quisling;

Edited by Erik Quisling
        p. cm.

ISBN-10: 1936965011
ISBN-13: 978-1936965014

Library of Congress

1. Clairvoyant / Psychic Development 2. Spiritual 3. New Age 4. Self-Help 5. Quisling, Tori

Upaya House Publishing
5120 River Road
Oakdale, CA 95361

Printed in USA

*This book is dedicated to my brother, Erik,
who has given me the vision and courage to keep
"throwing my hat over the wall."*

Contents

Dial the Root Chakra
Dial the Below the Navel Chakra
Dial the Stomach Chakra
Dial the Forehead Chakra
Dial Your Crown Chakra

The Two Clocks
Your Spirit and Your Physical Body
The Two Clocks Reading Technique
Prepare Yourself for the Reading.
Perform the Reading
End the Reading

Examples of "Two Clocks" Readings

Miracle Stories

The Clairvoyant Practitioner

Come with me
And you'll be
In a world of pure imagination.
Take a look
And you'll see
Into your imagination.
If you want to view paradise
Simply look around and view it
Anything you want to, do it.
Want to change the world?
There's nothing to it.

--Willy Wonka

Welcome!

Imagine your first trip to an amusement park or any other amazing experience that was magical to you. Your eyes are opened wide, your mouth open in awe and wonder.

This childlike awe and wonder is the state of imagination. When you open up your imagination, you open up your clairvoyance. This is what you will be developing in this book.

Clairvoyance is your psychic ability to see and know truths in life. Through clairvoyance, all the answers about anything at anytime are available to you.

We all possess limitless powers of imagination, and thus clairvoyance. However, most of us know very little about how to use either. From an early age we are taught to conform, and as we grow older, these

abilities naturally tend to get suppressed.
By consciously developing your clairvoyance, you will learn to reconnect with a great reservoir of power. You will notice yourself becoming more curious, playful, and courageous. You will find that you have the ability to tap into an omniscient quality inside of you that will open up potentials you never knew you had. Through this development, you will connect with who you are as a powerful being in a world of infinite possibilities.

Where do our imagination and clairvoyance come from?

When we imagine, visualize, or have a new idea, we are actually tapping into a subtle field of energy that lies just below the surface of our chaotic daily, physical reality. This subtle energy field is a well-organized array of frequencies that you can learn to tune in to just like finding the station on a radio. With a clear mind and focused attention, you can choose a frequency in which all information is stored on any particular topic – whether it be a person, an event, or a place.

So how do we tune in?

We are all familiar with terms like "I had a gut feeling," "I knew it off the top of my head," "my heart's not in it," "I can't see it happening," or "I have butterflies in my stomach." Notice how these phrases reference different parts of the body.

It just so happens that your clairvoyant abilities are located in these various parts of the body. In fact, these body parts are actually energy centers, called chakras, which are specially designed to detect all of the various frequencies of this subtle energy field.

Every person has these chakras. There are 11 chakras in total and together they form your body's Clairvoyant System.

It is the intention of this book to train you to be consciously aware of each chakra and to fully understand its specific area of focus.

Through this simple step-by-step guide, you will develop a heightened sense of "seeing" and "knowing" by learning to consciously tap into your Clairvoyant System. This conscious use of the Clairvoyant System is called a Reading.

By the end of this book you will know how to give a simple, yet powerful clairvoyant reading to another person as well as to yourself.

About Me

As a spiritually curious college student living in San Francisco in the 1980's, I found my way across the Bay to the Berkeley Psychic Institute (BPI), a school that specializes in developing clairvoyant abilities. It was founded by Lewis Bostwick, a man of immense wisdom and amusement. He also possessed a laser- sharp clairvoyance and when you spoke with him, it was as though he could see right through to your soul.

In his classes, we learned to communicate with neutrality and amusement in what were called aura readings. We used our clairvoyance to "see" spirit and create healings for all involved. We spoke our own language called "Beepineze." It sounded something like: "I got lit up on matching pictures, blew roses, turned down my analyzer and checked my grounding cord." My favorite phrase became: "Don't put that picture in my space!" People in my life not involved with BPI quickly learned the meaning of this.

During this time, I wrote articles for BPI's Psychic Reader Newspaper about power sites in San Francisco, as well as interviewed local channelers and healers. After I completed two years of training, I became the tour manager for BPI's Déjà Vu Tours, leading pilgrimages to spiritual sites and energy vortexes all over the world.

After Berkeley, I moved to New Orleans to work as a professional psychic and it was there that I created a House Healing business, making a living encountering poltergeists and strange energies in America's most haunted city. I also pursued my love of essential oils, leading courses on clairvoyant aromatherapy. But not long after these businesses began to take hold, I realized that my true passion in life was working with children. So I followed the path to becoming an elementary school teacher and went back to school where I earned teaching certifications as well as a Master's degree in Education.

As the new teacher to a classroom full of 5th graders, I quickly discovered that I could put my background in clairvoyance to use in the lesson plans. I developed exercises that allowed my students to effortlessly and unknowingly access their clairvoyant abilities in a fun and playful way.

As a fan of Lewis Carroll's Alice in Wonderland, I would tell my fifth and sixth grade students "to think of at least one impossible thing each day." Seeing beyond your reality is the first step in accessing your imagination. In my classroom, imagination and amusement were the most important means to growing and learning.

I became an expert guide to the imagination – encouraging thinking in divergent and creative ways. Nothing was impossible in my classroom. I created lessons of pure imagination called simulations. Through these simulations we "explored" the oceans to find gold, "landed" at Jamestown, "built" and met daily in a sweat lodge, "sailed" a ship in the SF Bay. The room smelled of the frankincense of old 17th Century Europe and the pine and drying vegetables of the colonial homes. I was not a teacher, but a clairvoyant guide to their highest creative selves!

Today, as founder of the New York Center for Clairvoyant Development, I have started my own school to teach the power of imagination and clairvoyance to people of all ages. Most of my students are adults, but I find that with a little training they quickly become kids again.

Through this book, I am honored to be your teacher and to help you develop your own clairvoyant tools. Ahead of you lies a magical way of being that offers all of the answers to what you are seeking as you make your way along your spiritual journey.

Part One:

The Clairvoyant System

THE HUMAN BODY'S CLAIRVOYANT SYSTEM

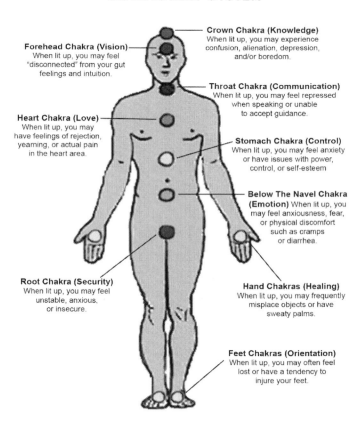

Crown Chakra (Knowledge)
When lit up, you may experience
confusion, alienation, depression,
and/or boredom.

Forehead Chakra (Vision)
When lit up, you may feel
"disconnected" from your gut
feelings and intuition.

Throat Chakra (Communication)
When lit up, you may feel repressed
when speaking or unable
to accept guidance.

Heart Chakra (Love)
When lit up, you may
have feelings of rejection,
yearning, or actual pain
in the heart area.

Stomach Chakra (Control)
When lit up, you may feel anxiety
or have issues with power,
control, or self-esteem

**Below The Navel Chakra
(Emotion)** When lit up, you
may feel anxiousness, fear,
or physical discomfort
such as cramps
or diarrhea.

Root Chakra (Security)
When lit up, you may feel
unstable, anxious,
or insecure.

Hand Chakras (Healing)
When lit up, you may frequently
misplace objects or have
sweaty palms.

Feet Chakras (Orientation)
When lit up, you may often feel
lost or have a tendency to
injure your feet.

The Clairvoyant System

Your body is a powerful instrument tuned in to receive information about the world on many levels. It not only has the five physical senses which include smelling, seeing, hearing, touching and tasting, it also has extra-senses tuned in to energy beyond the physical world. These extrasensory abilities, often called psychic abilities, are located in the chakras. Chakras, defined as "wheels" in the ancient Sanskrit language, are energy centers located throughout your body that spin, open, and close in response to various stimuli in the world around you.

Just as there are systems in your body such as the digestive system for processing food, the respiratory system for breathing air, and the sensory system for gathering stimuli in the physical world, there's an additional extra-sensory system to process the world beyond the five senses – it is a tightly connected network of chakras called the Clairvoyant System.

All told, there are eleven chakras operating within your Clairvoyant System. There are seven main chakras from the base of the spine to the top of your head, and one chakra in each hand and foot.

Each chakra behaves as a highly sophisticated sensor that tunes in to a different frequency of the world. Much in the same way our nose tunes into and recognizes the smell of fresh baked bread or our eyes tune into the face of a friend in a crowd, each chakra has its own area of specialization when tuning into information on a subconscious level. This information is then brought to our conscious awareness as a specific feeling within the body part that the chakra resides. By knowing each chakra's specialization, your clairvoyant system becomes a powerful tool for understanding the feelings that occur in any given situation.

For example, the phone rings a day after you interviewed for a job you really think you want. You notice that the area above your navel gives you a nervous feeling of anticipation. Moments later, the same area gives you a sinking feeling of disappointment when you find out it's a telemarketer instead.

As a clairvoyant, you acknowledge that this reaction is being felt strongly in your stomach chakra. By understanding that this chakra specializes in power and control issues, you realize you are losing your power to a circumstance that is out of your control. This conscious awareness then allows you to re-gain your neutrality and amusement and release the feelings from this chakra.

As in the example above, when the feeling in a chakra is particularly strong, that chakra is said to be "lit up." But once that chakra is acknowledged through your conscious awareness of what it is telling you, it then returns to its balanced "un-lit" state.

Oftentimes, however, this conscious awareness is never brought to a lit-up chakra. Instead we deny or resist the feelings broadcast by a particular chakra. Over long periods of time, if the unacknowledged feelings become too strong, they can be expressed by the body in the form of discomfort, weight gain, depression, or disease.

The Clairvoyant Center

How do we control our conscious awareness?

Conscious awareness is the specialization of the Forehead Chakra (commonly known as the 6th chakra.) Of all the chakras in the clairvoyant system, it is by far the most important because it allows acknowledgment of the other chakras to occur so they can return to their unlit state. In essence, the forehead chakra is like the bridge of your clairvoyant ship. It is a place where only neutrality and amusement can exist and as the captain of this bridge, you can only read the information coming in from the other chakras with neutrality and amusement. It is the most powerful place you can be present to and for this reason it is also known as your *Clairvoyant Center*.

Being present in your Clairvoyant Center allows you to be the observer in your life, separate from the drama of the events and situations. In this space you can easily remain neutral and amused – not losing yourself to reactions and emotional turmoil of your interactions. Here, you can stay aware of the chakras and the feelings they are causing while reading any situation.

For example, you may be having a conversation

with a friend who is confused about her life. You are feeling confused with her, and your area below the navel feels heavy. You remember your clairvoyant center and go up there. You see your friend as a capable, loving person, though afraid of change. When you allow yourself to tune-in or bring your awareness up to that spot of the Forehead chakra, you will find that your language changes in the conversation to seeing her distress as a response to change and growth. Your body now feels separate from this as you see that her situation is all part of something bigger in her life and that this will all work out.

In this Clairvoyant Center, you naturally achieve neutrality.

Neutrality, sometimes referred to as peace of mind, is the ability to experience an emotional state that is absent of emotion or judgment. It is a state of rest from the tension of thoughts and obligations in the world. In this state of neutrality, you experience a place of truth and clarity. You notice that peace is behind all situations and relationships with others. As you feel parts of your body "lighting up" with anxiety or tension, you can relieve these feelings and move forward by finding this place of neutrality and the truth that brings peace.

As you do this, your body no longer stores its extrasensory awareness as stories to tell yourself or others, creating anxious and worried feelings. Rather, these feelings are released or dissolved. Your body becomes a finely tuned instrument, a true assistant to your relationships, surroundings, and life goals.

From this Clairvoyant Center, you see beyond the problems and questions of life and see the peaceful nature and truth behind it all.

🔊)) **Note About Recordings:**

As a free companion to this book, I have recorded 24 guided meditations designed specifically to enhanced your clairvoyant development.

I recommend downloading all 24 into an MP3 player and then listening to each one when you are prompted with the "speaker symbol" at the end of each lesson. All recordings can be downloaded at the following link:

http://www.clairvoyantmeditation.com/book.php

Also, beneath each speaker symbol I have, in most cases, included a transcript of each guided meditation. Reading each transcript before listening to the recording can greatly enhance your experience.

Tuning In to your Clairvoyant Center

You can access your Clairvoyant Center very simply with your eyes open or closed. (Please read the complete instructions first so you can do the part of the activity that requires your eyes closed.)

To find your Clairvoyant Center, sit in a comfortable chair with your feet on the floor. Begin by lightly touching the center of your forehead just above your eyebrows. Smile and bring your attention to this area. *Then, close your eyes and gently roll them up to that spot on the forehead. Intend to bring your awareness to this spot as you open your eyes.*

 *__Find Your Clairvoyant Center__*

(http://www.clairvoyantmeditation.com/book.php)

You will find that your vision with your eyes open will also include this awareness of the Clairvoyant Center above the eyes. You may touch this spot on your forehead whenever you want to remind yourself of your Clairvoyant Center.

Consciously going to this spot will allow you to tune into a higher awareness of truth while being neutral. The more you find this area and use it, the more you gain strength just like an exercised muscle.

Your Chakras

As I describe each chakra, its location and abilities, imagine the feelings you have in each area of the body while staying in your clairvoyant center. You may touch that spot on your forehead periodically to remind yourself to be in this center.

Becoming consciously aware of these extra-senses for the first time can be like experiencing a new physical sense you haven't used such as your first vision after blindness or first smell after a clogged nose. These extra-senses have been there all along, you just haven't been using them with awareness.

Whenever you acknowledge or express the abilities in the chakras it makes them stronger.

Root Chakra -- Security

You are driving your car on a wet road, suddenly your wheels lose traction for a brief moment and you put on the brakes and slide. You regain traction and your place on the road but your senses are heightened, you have a pulling in your groin area and you are shaking.

The Root Chakra is located in the groin area.

When the Root Chakra opens wide or "lights up," you feel a rush of adrenaline, and feelings of anxiety and fear. Sometimes your body produces heat and will perspire and produce a blush in the cheeks.

The Root Chakra can light up if you or a loved one are physically threatened (i.e. nearly hurt in an accident) or conceptually threatened (i.e. news that the checking account is overdrawn; or you have to perform in front of an audience; or may be subject to embarrassment.) All have the same reaction in the body.

The Root Chakra is tuned into issues of survival, security, and family.

It is the place for grounding and a connection to our bodies and the physical plane. When balanced, we feel secure and safe. When blocked, we may feel unstable and anxious and insecure about the life we have created.

If this chakra becomes the dominant perspective of how one sees the world, a person may experience a fear and anxiety around most of life's experiences - especially ones that involve change. Their survival may depend strongly on things staying the same in a relationship. This person may also experience an inability to feel safe while driving or in social situations. The person may experience a jittery body, which doesn't allow the person to sit still or concentrate, as the body feels too unsafe. Physically, they may experience injuries or illness in the legs, knees, adrenal glands or kidneys as they experience a weak support system.

Taking inspired risks while being consciously grounded is one way to expand this chakra and begin to take control of it more fully. Inspired risks involve physical, social or spiritual changes.

The risky feeling that is coming from the Root Chakra is alerting you to your limitations. The inspiration is coming from your intuitive knowledge and desire to expand beyond these limiting beliefs. Consciously grounding while taking a risk can help keep you feeling secure.

People with a balanced Root Chakra have courage and confidence around risky situations, whether physical, social or spiritual.

For example, they are effective in situations of important life-saving decisions and may work as a fireman, emergency doctor, or military general. A person with a well-developed first chakra can also be a grounding force in creating a group of friends and maintaining a strong family or organization. They become someone whom others "ground through" or rely on for security. This person can also be attached to nature and all living beings on earth displaying tolerance and belief in the concept that "All is One."

Once you are aware that your Root Chakra is lighting up, you can learn to ground the fear-based, anxious feelings it is producing and read the energy of the situation.

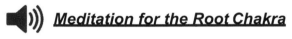

Meditation for the Root Chakra

(http://www.clairvoyantmeditation.com/book.php)

Sit in a comfortable chair with your feet on the floor. Close your eyes with a smile, and briefly touch the center of your forehead to locate your clairvoyant center.

Become aware of your tailbone settled in your chair. Imagine there is a spinning energy center just in front of the tailbone in the groin area facing straight down to the center of the earth. This is the root chakra.

When this chakra "lights up," it is telling you there are issues of security and survival. This chakra contains beliefs of your security that come not only from your own life experiences but from your family passed down from generation to generation. Imagine a color for this chakra and see it spinning.

As it spins watch the color get brighter and even change to a color that is more soothing and pleasing. As this new color comes into your root chakra, you are releasing the old fears and limiting beliefs about your security and survival. When you become more aware of this chakra, you naturally become more secure.

The root chakra can be a resource to let you know when you've encountered limiting beliefs about your security. To grow as a spirit you must move beyond these limiting beliefs from past experiences and family.

You realize that your own security does not depend on any one person, event or situation but rather on your connection to the earth which provides you with its constant gravitational support.

Below the Navel Chakra– Emotion

Your co-worker regularly discusses with you her worries and fears about her home situation. You care about her and share her worries and discuss the likelihood of her fears. You go home thinking about your co-worker's dilemma and feel a heaviness of worry and fear in the area below your navel. You feel that your own life is heavy and problematic as well.

Locate your Below the Navel Chakra (also called the 2nd chakra) by placing two fingers horizontally under your navel. It is located between the Root Chakra and the navel.

The Below the Navel Chakra is related to emotion and relationships with the psychic ability of clairsentience, or the ability to feel what others feel.

This chakra allows you to match the emotions of others and identify with these emotions as your own. With this ability, you can take on others' emotions they are experiencing and allow them to feel better or healed. When you see someone crying, you begin crying. You may go from happy and content to sad and unsettled when you hear the news of someone else's misfortune.

This is the emotion of sympathy or taking on the feelings of others. When this chakra stays open too often, you may become very sensitive and overwhelmed by crowded places.

For a person in the role as healer, therapist, or close friend, this works well as long as the emotions you take on remain separate from your own and are released. Otherwise, the emotions can quickly build up in this area of the body and become part of your own problems to solve.

When the Below the Navel Chakra lights up, you may feel tension in that area, excitement, anxiousness, fear or have discomfort, cramps or even diarrhea. The abdominal area can become bloated and often the appetite is affected – either overeating or not eating at all to calm the area.

This chakra is quite reactive and can make you feel out of control with excitement, hysteria, or irritability.

The Below the Navel Chakra lights up when you are attached emotionally to someone or a situation involving a relationship.This is the area of relationships and emotional security. This can be a sexual attachment or someone you care for deeply and have taken on much of their emotions.

A person who sees the world through this chakra may need to control others in relationships. They may be meddling and interfering and be more concerned with others' lives than their own. Since money has to do with relationships, the person may have fear around making or losing money. A person may experience insecurity about sexuality and struggle with uncontrollable desire or jealousy.

Once aware of the Below the Navel chakra lighting up, you realize you have taken in the emotions of another person. You can learn to let go of these foreign emotions, calm your body and gain amusement over your own emotional well-being.

Meditation for the Below the Navel Chakra

(http://www.clairvoyantmeditation.com/book.php)

Sit in a comfortable chair with your feet on the floor. Close your eyes with a smile and briefly touch the center of your forehead to locate your clairvoyant center.

Place your hand over your abdomen just below the navel. This is your Below the Navel chakra.

When this chakra "lights up" it is telling you there are issues of emotional attachment. This chakra holds beliefs about responsibility for others and holds the ability of clairsentience, matching any emotions around.

Allow your thoughts to go to any problems or people that come up as you become aware of this chakra. Notice the color of this chakra. Imagine there are lines of energy connecting you to these problems and people. Be amused at the number of them.

Gently pull each of these lines out from the Below the Navel chakra and watch them disappear.

Watch the chakra spin free of these connections

and take on a new healing color.

You realize that your own emotions are manageable and calm and that any problems that originate from you are easy to solve.

Stomach Chakra – Control

You are driving across town to meet someone for lunch. On your way, you feel happy and satisfied. All of a sudden you begin to get a worried and anxious feeling in your stomach area – above the navel. You see that you have a text message and the person you are meeting is already there a little early and is wondering where you are. You rush and feel frustrated that this person is expecting you already. You forget about your easygoing thoughts and feel pressured and rushed.

The Stomach Chakra is located above the navel and directly below the ribcage in the stomach area. Also called the 3rd chakra or Solar Plexus, it is located in the center of the body.

When the Stomach Chakra "lights up," you experience feelings of tension, anxiety, energy level fluctuations, effort, and force in the stomach area. The issues associated with this chakra are power, control, will, and self-esteem.

When this chakra is balanced, you can set goals and stick to them. You experience hunches or gut feelings in this chakra that feel positive or negative and you have certainty in following internal directions from these feelings.

A person who experiences the world through the Stomach Chakra may be in frequent fear, struggle, or exhaustion. The person may either want to eat more to feel better or lose their appetite and not eat at all. People often develop ulcers, acid reflux and a distended belly, which looks especially strange in men. The person feels the need to give people advice and often attempts to control that person. This person may also feel controlled by others. The person may have trouble sleeping or staying asleep. This person may ignore their hunches and rely on others for guidance.

When hunches are followed, this chakra gets stronger and the level of self-esteem grows. As this ability grows, you can experience an increased sense of power and belief in accomplishing your goals. Clarity in this chakra allows you to feel powerful. You can also easily detach from others' drama and problems.

Meditation for the Stomach Chakra

(http://www.clairvoyantmeditation.com/book.php)

Sit in a comfortable chair with your feet on the floor. Close your eyes with a smile and briefly touch the center of your forehead to locate your clairvoyant center.

Place your hand over your stomach-area, just below the ribcage. This is the stomach chakra (above the Navel and below the ribcage.)

When this chakra "lights up" it is telling you there are issues of control and power. This chakra hold beliefs about authority, judgment and self-worth. It is your energy source to create something new in your life. Become aware of any tension or tightness.

Make a laugh and send amusement to that area. Notice the tension you feel in that area sitting right under the laughter. Much of the energy left behind in this chakra feels like judgment, guilt and fear. Imagine that there is a small sun located right in front of the stomach chakra.

Imagine that this sun has the power to absorb any tension that you feel there and transform it into pure life force energy. Take in a deep breath. When you breathe out, you send all this tension into the gold sun.

Do this 3 more times. Breathe in, Breathe out. Watch the sun get bigger and brighter. Breathe in, Breathe out. Watch the sun get even bigger and brighter. Breathe in, Breathe out. Watch the sun get much bigger and brighter. Imagine that the sun has absorbed the tension and transformed it into pure light. All the judgment is neutralized. Reach out and bring that gold sun directly into your third chakra as a pure life force energy and power.

You realize that you are the most powerful in your world. All decisions come from you and you are responsible for all you create. You are eager to make your dreams a reality.

Heart Chakra – Love

You walk into a restaurant and realize your friends have created a surprise party for you. The room is filled with your dearest friends. There is a pulling feeling in your heart and you can't stop smiling. You feel welcome and accepted. A sense of deep appreciation radiates from your chest and your eyes fill with tears.

The Heart Chakra is located at the sternum in the center of the chest. Also called the 4th chakra, it contains the abilities of love, compassion, forgiveness, and commitment.

When the Heart chakra lights up you may have feelings of love or discomfort, rejection, yearning, depression, or actual pain in the heart area. Issues included in this chakra are about self-acceptance in relationships and your place in the world often associated with rejection.

This chakra lights up when the issue is deeply important to your soul and your spiritual well-being.

When balanced, we feel compassion and have a deep sense of peace, centeredness, and purpose. When out of balance, this chakra leads to bitterness, greed, depression, and difficulty with forgiveness.

When a person sees the world through this chakra, they may convey neediness. For some people, connecting to others in the heart area can be a matter of life and death and can feel extreme. This person may be eager to please and do anything to make you a friend. This person needs constant reassurance as if their survival depends on you liking them. This behavior will often push people away as they resist the responsibility it takes to avoid hurting this person's feelings or causing them anxiety.

Many addictions come from an imbalance of this chakra which results in a lack of loving yourself. A person needs to find love externally. This person is overly concerned with how others feel or think of them; their love of self depends on the reactions of others.

They often feel victimized by others and use this victim mentality to get attention. They are unable to let go of old resentments and allowing others to love them.

For anyone, it takes some practice and training to gain awareness of your ability to love oneself and feel whole and complete by yourself.

🔊 _**Meditation for the Heart Chakra**_

(http://www.clairvoyantmeditation.com/book.php)

Sit in a comfortable chair with your feet on the floor. Close your eyes with a smile and briefly touch the center of your forehead to locate your clairvoyant center.

Place your hand over your heart. This is the heart chakra.

When the heart chakra "lights up," it is telling you there are issues of love, purpose, commitment and forgiveness in the situation.

Notice how open or closed, heavy or light, your heart feels. Often there are openings in the heart chakra – like holes or outlets – seeking for others to plug in. There is a neediness there – a sense of unfulfillment or unfinished business.

Imagine you can feel or see your favorite color penetrating your heart from the inside and expanding outward, filling in the holes and dissolving all the fears and restrictions that have been occupying this center.

Imagine that the heart chakra is spinning, whole and complete.

Your heart is now open to receive love through generosity rather than need. The word "yes" is written across your heart. You can have more joy, appreciation, and deep love for yourself and others.

Throat Chakra – Communication

You approach your boss to discuss a better position and increased salary. You believe you are worth more and deserve more recognition. As you are ready to speak your truth, your throat feels painfully tight and as you speak, you must clear your throat of phlegm that arises. It's even hard to breathe through this constriction in the throat. As you begin speaking, and the boss is listening, your throat opens and you relay confidence and conviction.

The Throat Chakra (also called the 5th chakra) is located at the base of the throat in the thyroid area and includes channels in the jaw and sinuses in the face. The Throat Chakra is related to communication, speaking your truth, inner voice and creativity.

When the Throat Chakra lights up, it feels like a knot or tightness in the throat, sometimes with phlegm, which can make it hard to speak, either with strained voice or not at all.

This is the communication center often used for mediumship – communicating with entities beyond the physical realm using the psychic ability, clairaudience.

Clairaudience is the ability to tune-in, hear or speak with spirits that don't have physical bodies. These spirits can be spirit guides, angels, passed relatives (yours or someone near you), or future children called "baby beings."

When the Throat Chakra is developed, it is easy to hear guidance from your inner voice and have the faith to follow it.

Telepathy, the ability to communicate silently with other people or animals, is also present in this chakra. A developed Throat Chakra allows you to be fully expressive and heal through communication and creative endeavors.

When the Throat Chakra is out of balance, blockages in this area can lead to problems with the throat and sinuses, including sore throat, colds, stiff neck, hearing problems and thyroid problems. A person will often repress speaking their truth or listening to guidance. The person doubts or overrides inner messages to communicate or take action and lets others define their needs and wants.

The Heart and Throat Chakras form the base of your creative channels.

Your soul's purpose is in your heart and your truth is

in your throat. These get expressed through channels in your shoulders and arms and they manifest out into the world through your hands. When these areas are restricted, so is your creative expression.

Meditation for the Throat Chakra

(http://www.clairvoyantmeditation.com/book.php)

Sit in a comfortable chair with your feet on the floor. Close your eyes with a smile and briefly touch the center of your forehead to locate your clairvoyant center.

Place your hand over the base of your throat. This is your throat chakra. When the Throat Chakra "lights up," it is telling you there are issues of expression and communication involved.

Notice if your throat feels tight or relaxed. We connect with others through this area whether they are in our presence or far away. It is here that you use your telepathic ability to speak your thoughts directly to another person with whom you have agreed to connect.

Become aware of these connections you have made with the people in your life – even groups or communities. Feel the "cords" or lines that connect you to all of them.

Imagine them as luminous fibers pulling on your throat as they light up with thoughts, ideas and requests of others. Take note of the number of people – sometimes this number can be very large! Recognize yourself as a great communicator.

Imagine that you can see the outlet that the "cords" are plugged into. Use your hand to gently but forcefully pull the cords out of the outlet and intend for these cords to dissolve as the connection is unplugged. Imagine your Throat Chakra filling with golden light and becoming whole and complete and free of cords. Let yourself enjoy the silence so that your true inner voice can be revealed.

Forehead Chakra – Vision

*(1) You are walking down some stairs in front of some
important people. You imagine falling down the stairs
and feel fear of this embarrassing vision. You take the
next step and fall down the stairs. You just fell into your
own vision. The next time you go down the same stairs
you notice the falling "picture" again. This time you
smile and intend to do it differently and not fall.*

*(2) You have a job interview. You hear that the
competition is stiff and they are looking for an
experienced person. Rather than worry, you imagine the
room with the people who are hiring you. You see them
laughing and eager to meet you. They are shaking your
hand and welcoming you. They are saying "We really
like you. When can you start?" You are excited later
when this vision comes true.*

*(3) Your friend describes her financial condition as being
"stuck in a corner" with her current job. She complains
of the pay, the co-workers, her bosses and the commute.
You see your friend's darkness and her desperation as
she hits up against walls and suffers from lack of choices
and being stuck. It is a difficult vision to look at because
you see that she is so creative and with so much potential.
Instead of advice, you tell your friend that you see her
free with so many choices. As you "tune in" to her
choices you notice her talent for communication and see*

her working from her own desk at home with an abundance of clients calling and personal satisfaction. You share this vision with her. She sees it with you and feels excited at the possibilities you see with her.

The Forehead Chakra is located in the center of the forehead above the eyebrows. The Forehead Chakra governs the act of seeing, both physically and clairvoyantly.

When the Forehead Chakra lights up, it doesn't generate feeling or emotions in the area of the body like the other chakras, rather the other parts of the body react to the pictures it creates.

You may experience tightness or pressure in the forehead area when you are overwhelmed by what you see. When the Forehead Chakra lights up, you may experience flashes of images, ideas, or thoughts as you are encountering a person or situation.

This information comes from your imagination of possibilities and truths.

Often a scary image is just a fear you are detecting, while an image that inspires you is a truth. It just depends on which image or thought you put your attention.

The psychic abilities in this chakra are clairvoyance and precognition.

Clairvoyance means "to see the truth" and this truth usually appears in the forms of pictures, symbols, and colors.

Clairvoyance is the key to tuning in to all your abilities and balancing your spirit and body.

Precognition is the ability to see the future or follow a trajectory of where a person or situation is headed. Precognition can also be used as a tool for envisioning a clear picture of what you desire, overriding any patterns that are creating your current reality now.

When the Forehead Chakra is balanced, thinking is clear and the vision is strong. When out of balance, one feels disconnected from their intuition or "gut" feelings.

When in tune with the Forehead Chakra, a person can see chakras, auras, spirit guides and other forms that allow them to gaze inside the soul and capture the essence of a person. From this chakra, you will naturally see images of past and future.

With this chakra open, you can visualize a future and manifest a life you would like to live. Once the Forehead Chakra is under control, you may see a vision of falling down the stairs and use a technique to immediately let the vision go – bringing amusement rather than fear in the body; thereby avoiding the fall.

A person who has an imbalanced or overly active forehead chakra will see many pictures randomly around them. They may say whatever comes to mind even if it's inappropriate or easily offends others. They may also be in fear of what they see since they don't understand what is happening.

Sometimes that person resists or denies their own clairvoyance since they believe they are responsible for what they see. When the Forehead Chakra is shut down, a person loses all ability to imagine. They over-intellectualize and are guided solely by linear facts found in the material world.

Meditation for the Forehead Chakra

(http://www.clairvoyantmeditation.com/book.php)

Sit in a comfortable chair with your feet on the floor. Close your eyes with a smile and briefly touch the center of your forehead to locate your clairvoyant center. Keep your hand on your forehead. This is the forehead chakra.

When the forehead chakra "lights up," you are using your vision to see the truth or possible future events. Notice if there is darkness here or colors and light. Often when we put our attention on this area there will be a person's face or a vision of something you are trying to solve or understand.

Imagine that this spot on your forehead is a headlamp such as the kind on a coal miner's hat. You can reach up and turn it off and go into darkness or turn it on and shine a light out in front of you. Notice if the light is bright or dull. Take an imaginary cloth in your hand and shine up the light, clean off the debris, mud and dust.

Now see the light as focused and clear. You can play with the light – making it a narrow focus or a broad focus. You can turn it on or off whenever you like. It is your ability to see in the dark. Just because you see doesn't mean you are responsible for what appears before you.

Allow yourself to be a detached observer, curious and amused. Allow all the things that show up in this light to be merely illusions that you may adjust.

This is the place of your imagination. It is important to clean and use it often to allow your vision to get stronger and more powerful.

Crown Chakra – Knowledge

(1) You put together a party and are in charge of more than 100 people. You are surveying the guests and the room to make sure everyone is doing well. You feel and emulate a sense of authority and importance that people notice. You feel a definite pressure on top of your head. When the guests leave, you feel relief from the pressure in the top of your head and feel satisfied with a job well-done.

(2) You unexpectedly are asked to speak in front of a room full of people. You have to act quickly and what comes out of your mouth is eloquent and insightful. The audience cheers. You can only be amazed by what came off the top of your head without a plan.

The Crown Chakra, also called the 7th chakra, is located on the top of the head. Rub the top of your head and feel the warm spot there.

The abilities contained in this chakra allow access to your own certainty, wisdom and knowing, often called the Higher Self.

The Crown Chakra contains the psychic abilities of

Certainty and Knowing. With these abilities, you can have an air of authority about your communication even if you don't know what's going on.

Others will trust and follow you. This ability works well for a teacher, supervisor, or other leader. With certainty, you can trust that the answer will be available when needed.

You may often experience the feeling that the information just comes through you.
The Crown Chakra also contains the psychic ability of trance-mediumship that allows your spirit to leave the body or channel another entity through. You can use this ability to feel others' emotions deeply, become like them, and sometimes even talk like them. Many actors and comedians are excellent trance-mediums.

When developed, the top of the head chakra brings us knowledge, wisdom, understanding, spiritual connection and bliss.

When out of balance, there may be an inability to learn, confusion, apathy, alienation, depression and/or boredom.

Meditation for the Crown Chakra

(http://www.clairvoyantmeditation.com/book.php)

Sit in a comfortable chair with your feet on the floor. Close your eyes with a smile and briefly touch the center of your forehead to locate your clairvoyant center.

Place your hand on the top of your head. Notice the warm spot there. This is your top of the head chakra or Crown Chakra.

When this chakra "lights up," you are connecting with the part of you that is infinite and unrestricted. Often you are accessing important information that you need to feel smart or there is a situation that is difficult for your spirit to handle and you feel disoriented.

Imagine there is a hat on your head of your favorite color that makes you feel happy and smart. Wear this hat proudly and check in with this hat during the day to make sure it is still there. This is your certainty and attitude. The hat also keeps you present and aware of what is going on even if you are uncomfortable in a situation.

The more you practice looking for your hat and keeping it on your head, the more you stay present and accessing your higher knowledge.

Hand Chakras -- Healing

Rub your hands together and feel the heat generated. Pull the palms of your hands slightly apart from each other and continue to feel the sensation that is present. This is your energy coming from the chakras contained in the palms of the hands. You may even see white circles form in the palms as you pay attention to them. These chakras generate heat and act as sensors to feel energy.

You have at least five psychic abilities just in your hands. The hand chakras have the main abilities to heal and create. Healing is simply the act of moving stuck energy. You can heal by sending loving heat through the hands as a massage therapist, while you can create things in material form as an artist. On more advanced awareness levels, you can channel a spirit or energy source through the hands to perform magnetic or reiki healings.

Two other abilities located in the hands are psychometry, the ability to read the energy or images by holding an object, and telekinesis, a rare ability to move or bend objects without touching them.

If there is an imbalance in the Hand Chakras, you

may have a high ability to heal others but you may experience sweaty hands and energy drain around sick people since you are unconsciously giving away your healing energy to those around you. If you have a high telekinetic ability, you may lose your keys or misplace objects frequently (when really you are moving them without knowing it) as well as "blowing out" light bulbs and electronics.

 ### *Meditation for the Hand Chakras*

(http://www.clairvoyantmeditation.com/book.php)

Sit in a comfortable chair with your feet on the floor. Close your eyes with a smile and briefly touch the center of your forehead to locate your clairvoyant center. Rest your hands on your lap with the palms facing upward.

Imagine your hands are heavy as if each is holding a weighted ball in the center of the palms. As the palms of your hands sink into your legs, you feel them widening and spinning. Imagine there is a beam of light coming out of each palm shining straight up to the sky.

Notice the power you have in your hands to create, heal and channel energy and intentions. Turn your hands toward each other with the palms facing but not touching. Imagine the light beams mixing together, confirming the power located there. Imagine them spinning and clear of responsibility, free to create something completely new.

Shake your hands out and rub them together. The hand chakras are now energized.

Feet Chakras – Orientation (Earth)

You are visiting a new city for the first time. Rather than ride in a car, you walk for hours through the streets absorbing the feeling of the culture and people who live there. Your feet are sore; but you feel you really know this new place.

The chakras in the feet are located in the arches of each foot. They contain the ability to tune in to earth energy and specifically the attitudes, culture and safety of your location. The feet chakras orient you to the surroundings and your place on earth.

People naturally release the energy of their thoughts and feelings into the ground which the Feet Chakras register. When traveling to a different time zone, you can ease jet lag by allowing the feet to bring in the energy of the new place in which you have arrived.

You can use your feet chakras to absorb earth energy from deep below the surface with just an intention to heal the body and specifically the energy channels in the legs. The Feet Chakras give you confidence to move forward in life as well as establish your stability in present time. A person with Feet Chakras that are imbalanced may frequently injure their feet and feel unsure of their next move in their lives.

Meditation for the Feet Chakras

(http://www.clairvoyantmeditation.com/book.php)

Sit in a comfortable chair with your feet on the floor. Close your eyes with a smile and briefly touch the center of your forehead to locate your clairvoyant center.

Notice your feet planted on the floor. Become aware of the arches of your feet spinning. These are your feet chakras.

Notice that these chakras are pulling up energy under them. Imagine that this energy is pure, natural earth energy.

Send your imagination deep into the earth away from the surface chaos where you find gentle steam vents. These gentle steam vents blow up into your feet chakras and cleanse and clear them of any heaviness or stuck energy.

Your feet are now ready to take in the healing that the earth provides and orient you firmly to the earth.

Part Two:

Find Your Space

The 7 Tools To Find Your Space

By now, you've learned about your chakras and you understand what they are telling you. You are familiar with the different abilities in each chakra and can "tune in" to the feelings they "light up" in your body.

Each time a feeling lights up, you can bring your attention to your Clairvoyant Center and acknowledge the information your chakras are giving you.

The next step is to develop tools to release these sensations.

Each tool is part of a meditation called "Find Your Space." It is essential that you perform this meditation before conducting any type of clairvoyant reading.

Each tool of the "Find Your Space" meditation can be used alone to give you more energy, as well as create boundaries and protection in your daily life.

Each tool is designed to help you release the discomfort or "lit up" feeling from your chakras. They will also help prevent you from feeling lit up in the first place and ultimately prepare you to do a clairvoyant reading as you separate your energy and beliefs from those around you.

It is best to learn each tool completely before you do the final "Find Your Space" meditation.

Tool #1: Find Your Clairvoyant Center

To find your Clairvoyant Center, sit in a comfortable chair with your feet on the floor. Begin by lightly touching the center of your forehead just above your eyebrows.   Smile and bring your attention to this area. Then, close your eyes and gently roll them up to that spot on the forehead.

Intend to bring your awareness to this spot as you open your eyes. You will find that your vision with your eyes open will also include this awareness of the clairvoyant center above the eyes. You may touch this spot on your forehead whenever you want to remind yourself of your Clairvoyant Center.

This spot, also called the Forehead Chakra, is your place of clairvoyance and your ability to see clearly. Going to this spot will allow you to tune into a higher awareness of truth while being neutral. The more you find this area and use it, the more you gain strength - just like an exercised muscle.

 **_Find Your Clairvoyant Center_**

(http://www.clairvoyantmeditation.com/book.php)

Tool #2: Find Your Amusement

Sit in a comfortable chair with your feet on the floor.

Close your eyes with a smile and briefly touch the center of your forehead to locate your Clairvoyant Center.

Notice the areas of your body that are serious or heavy. Smile at each of these places. When you breathe out, compress your belly in a deep laugh – "ha ha." Continue to breathe, smile, and laugh deeply until it comes out naturally.

Imagine with each laugh the energy is releasing. The smile on your face tells your body it is okay to release the stuck feeling and move on.

When you are amused, you are in charge (and senior to) anything or anyone in your life.

 _**Find Your Amusement**_

(http://www.clairvoyantmeditation.com/book.php)

Tool #3: Grounding Cord – Harnessing Gravity

Our bodies naturally build up an electrical charge from all the energy absorbed from thoughts, people, situations, and the mechanical world. This excess charge feels like anxiety, doubt, fear, and worry. A Grounding Cord connects you with the gravity at the core of the earth to effortlessly pull away this excess charge.

When the body gives you an emotion that is uncomfortable, you imagine it going down the Grounding Cord into the center of the earth. A Grounding Cord not only allows you to release any excess energy, it also opens up spaces in the body for more of your own light and answers to flow through you. You feel energized. As a grounded person, you are able to deal with a difficult situation or person in a responsive rather than reactive manner. Your sense of humor is easy to find and you can remain calm in the midst of an emotional crisis.

You can also notice how places such as businesses and houses are affected by grounding. For example, the people working in a grounded office are friendly, organized, and efficient. It is easy to find your way around and you feel relaxed. On the other hand, you may notice an ungrounded place to be hectic, confusing, and unpleasant.

As you become more familiar with the grounding technique for yourself and the room, you can begin to ground places in general. You can ground your workplace, your car, or your home. You will find that any frenetic energy and chaos will dissipate when you have consciously grounded a space – preferably before you arrive. You can also ground objects, children, and pets. Before grounding your body, it is important to ground the room where you are sitting to make it a safe place and to more easily focus.

 ### **_Create a Grounding Cord_**

(http://www.clairvoyantmeditation.com/book.php)

Sit in a comfortable chair with your feet on the floor. Close your eyes with a smile and briefly touch the center of your forehead to locate your clairvoyant center. Imagine a golden bubble of light surrounding the room.

Imagine the room is filled with this golden light and suspended and separate from other places nearby. Know that the room is safe and no one will be entering.

Next, imagine there is a large hollow beam of light coming up through the floor –shooting up through the room into the ceiling and out the roof. You notice that it is coming from the center of the Earth and it is filled with gravity. This is called a grounding cord. You notice it is highly magnetic because it is pulling all forms of energy to it – you feel any heaviness leave your body and the space around your body. Anything that may be sticking to you or making you feel heavy is flying into this center column.

Also, you see that all four corners of the room have beams of light connected to this center grounding cord so the room is contained and filled with movement and light.

Intend and say the following (in your head or out-loud): All energies and beings not in agreement with the high level of communication and growth intended in this room are now going down the grounding cord.

With your eyes closed and a smile, notice where your thoughts are right now. Become aware of the chair you are sitting in and the room you are sitting in. Notice if there are parts of your body that are speaking to you. Take note of the parts that speak to you and the feelings or emotions you perceive.

Notice these are the places you hold energy in your body.

Next, become aware of your chair and its support. Feel the base of your spine connecting with the chair. In your groin area is your root chakra. It is spinning and open.

Imagine another hollow beam coming up from the center of the earth through the floor, but this time right under your chair. It comes up through the chair and plugs in to your root chakra – completely and effortlessly.

Allow any of the discomfort in your body to effortlessly be pulled through this hollow cord by gravity to the center of the earth. The gravity is intelligently pulling all the discomfort out. The earth simply transforms this energy and returns it to its source.

As you breathe, know that your life force energy is coming into your body and filling in the open spaces.

Any doubt or worry goes down the grounding cord. Notice that people and colors are going down - it can grow wide to accommodate all that is leaving your body.

Tool #4: Energy Fountains

Now that you have your Grounding Cord as a way to release excess energy and settle your body and the room, you are ready to clear your energy channels in the lower and upper parts of your body. Your body is completely supported by the Earth below and the cosmic energy above.

The Earth energy supports your foundation and direction on the planet. It allows you to experience the physical form. Your Feet Chakras connect with and read this Earth energy. On the surface, this Earth energy can be uncomfortable, prickly or stressful, reflecting people and cars especially in an urban area.

When you purposely create a flow between the earth and the sky, you allow your body to be a conduit. This flow is a form of cleansing and protection, nothing can stick to you. In this energy flow, you become a presence rather than a person. You lose your shape and form and sit in the flow.

Imagine sitting in the center of a beautiful fountain that cleanses you from the inside out.

Some people who travel or have emigrated from a different country will find that their time is all off –

they are still running Earth energy from that country. Consciously running the Earth energy of the place where your body is located helps travelers with jet lag . The body, with the spirit's help, will run the appropriate time of that part of the Earth and become adjusted faster.

Running Your Energy

(http://www.clairvoyantmeditation.com/book.php)

Sit in a comfortable chair with your feet on the floor. Close your eyes with a smile and briefly touch the center of your forehead to locate your clairvoyant center.

Become aware of your grounding cord and your feet resting on the floor.
Notice the arches of your feet have a tingling or tension in them. These are the feet chakras, which are especially created to connect your body with the earth giving you stability and direction.

Imagine the energy of the earth as soothing steam vents coming up into your feet from a mile down where it is clean and healing. Also notice if it is earth energy from another place other than from where you are currently sitting.

Observe the earth energy running up the legs, through the hips and looping down through the grounding cord in the root chakra.

The grounding cord in your root chakra creates the suction of this lower body energy loop. Your lower body should feel rooted into your seat. Sometimes energy starts to dislodge from the legs, especially the hips, allow this energy to go down the grounding cord. Any sensations you begin to feel in the body only validate the energy work you are actually doing.

Lightly rub the spot on top of your head – your crown chakra – and feel the warmth of this spot. It is especially tuned to bring in cosmic energy.
Bring your awareness to the space high above our earth's atmosphere – into the cosmos. The energy is very clear.

Notice there is a grid of light full of wisdom and non-judgment. Allow the energy from this place to flow into the top of your head. You may see a color or several colors as it comes in through the top of your head and down the back energy channel along the spine. As it runs down the spine, notice the chakras that go through your back and how they are spinning.

This cosmic energy pools in the first chakra and mixes with the earth energy there, then comes up the front channels of the body, spouting as a fountain out the top of your head. Put your attention on the fountain – see any colors – see its strength as it pours through your aura, healing your space.

Clear the Creative Channels. Now begin to notice that some of that cosmic energy coming up your front channels is pooling in the center of your chest, in your heart chakra. It is going out the sides of your chest into the creative arm channels and out the hands. Place your hands on your lap with the palms up. You notice there are now fountains spouting out the palms of the hands or hand chakras.

It is also pooling in the base of your throat, in the throat chakra moving through your shoulders and down the arm channels mixing with the energy out the hands, strengthening the fountains out the hands. Just keep observing the fountains out the top of the head chakra and the hands and know your energy is running.

At any time, allow any effort or uncertainty about seeing or experiencing these tools to go down the grounding cord.

Tool #5: Aura Bubble and the Protection Rose

You are an immense and limitless being. Only a small part of your spirit can fit inside your body at one time. This part of you that does not fit into the body forms an energetic body of light called your aura. It is intricate, alive and complex. Shamans have described the aura as a matrix of light which holds energy as thoughts and visions.

All of your soul's answers are in this energetic light body that surrounds you.

The aura is very flexible, moving like an elastic balloon. We spread our auras out through our awareness. So whatever you are aware of right now while reading this you have in your aura. With a thought, you can pull your aura in like an elastic balloon around your body. As your aura comes in closer to your body it becomes more concentrated and contained and your vibration is raised.

You are responsible for everything in your aura. So besides your physical body in your chair right now, you are also responsible for all other things contained in the aura. You bring these things and other people into your aura when you become aware or think about them.

An easy way to bring your aura in and remind yourself about "your space" is to imagine a rose in front of you that is fixed on the edge of your aura.

You can find this by holding your hand in front of your face and pretend it is a hand mirror. Pull your hand back to the distance that you would be able to properly see yourself. This should be about a half an arms length away.

Imagine that the hand mirror has now become a beautiful rose out in front of you. This rose, which stays fixed in front of you, shows you the edge of your aura.

It travels as quickly as your thoughts. So with a thought have the rose move way out in the distance to a tiny dot – your aura grows large. Move it back in close to you and your aura moves in around your body again.

Tell the rose to move around your entire aura leaving a neon blue trail of light. Watch how it instantly creates this neon blue light surrounding your aura. Now you are sitting in blue light and the rose is out in front of you. This rose is set to absorb energy and moves around intelligently knowing where energy is coming in. The rose out in front of you is your way of knowing that your aura is pulled in around you. It pulls your entire aura in with it.

By watching the rose as you speak with someone you stay in your body. You don't go out to that person or somewhere in the room. Seeing this rose close in front of you will allow you to quickly pull in your aura and be "in your space." You may find it helpful to keep this rose out in front of you while you speak with people in person or on the phone. You stay behind the rose and in your space. The rose absorbs what the person is saying so you can listen and stay neutral to the conversation.

This Rose allows you to be aware, in your space and pulls your aura in around you. When you are inside your aura and contained – you are at your brightest and most concentrated and powerful. By thinking of your rose, you instantly bring the aura in around you for protection and power. Before walking into a building or answering the phone – see your rose.

Find the Edge of Your Aura

(http://www.clairvoyantmeditation.com/book.php)

Sit in a comfortable chair with your feet on the floor. Close your eyes with a smile and briefly touch the center of your forehead to locate your clairvoyant center. Become aware of your energetic self surrounding you. Imagine that it is a large balloon that is elastic. With just a thought, bring it into the room where you are sitting. Define your aura around you by holding your arms out straight and moving your arms in the following way:

Put your arms out straight in front of you. Imagine that the edge of your aura is at the tip of your fingers. Raise your arms straight up to the ceiling to find the top of your aura. Drop your arms like straight wings to the sides of your body to find the sides of your aura.

Raise your arms again and drop them straight behind you (imagine you are flexible) to define the back of your aura. Bend down and imagine sweeping your straight arms under your feet to define the bottom of your aura and sit up again.

Now see yourself as having an egg of light surrounding you at an arm's length.

Tool #6: Find the Room in the Center of Your Head

The area behind your eyes is your viewing place where there are no emotions. It is easy to be neutral and amused in this area of the body.

It is important to become familiar and comfortable with this area in your head. It gives you direct access to your clairvoyance and viewing screen.

 Find Your Room in the Center of Your Head

(http://www.clairvoyantmeditation.com/book.php)

Sit in a comfortable chair with your feet on the floor. Close your eyes with a smile and briefly touch the center of your forehead to locate your clairvoyant center.

With a smile, touch the front of you forehead with one hand and the back of your head with the other hand.

The place between your hands is called the center of your head.

Imagine that there is a room in there with a small white light.
You begin to notice that this white light is steadily growing in the center of your head.

It has grown to the size of a golf ball and continues to expand.
Notice that you feel relaxed as you watch this white light – no thoughts can penetrate this white light.
As it grows, you also notice that anything in its path gets dissolved in the white light. It has reached your scalp and has now moved beyond to create a white halo around your head.

You relax in this white light, as thoughts come to you they don't penetrate as you rest in this white light.
Now you notice it is shrinking and has returned to its original size in the center of your head.

The white light has left behind open space and you can clearly see a room now in the center of your head.
The room here is a place of serenity.

Make it your own with your favorite colors, textures

and surroundings, including plants and even a beautiful view.

Laugh and dance wildly around in the room letting the entire world know this is your room. You may even choose to write your name on the walls.

Create a comfortable chair in that room and sit down.

Tool #7: Fill up with a Gold Sun

Now that you've released so much energy you must replenish these open spaces with your own highest creative life force energy. You may use this whenever you feel depleted and need more inspired energy. After the Gold Sun recording, you will be ready to Find Your Space!

 __Fill Up with a Gold Sun__

(http://www.clairvoyantmeditation.com/book.php)

Sit in a comfortable chair with your feet on the floor. Close your eyes with a smile and briefly touch the center of your forehead to locate your clairvoyant center.

Imagine there is a large gold magnet over your head with your name on it. It is pulling back all of your highest creative life force energy from all the people, places, events, situations, future, and past that you've left it. It has formed into a beautiful, bright golden sun over your head that grows larger and larger. It is so bright that you need sunglasses to look up at it. It is sparkling with enthusiasm, joy and amusement.

Reach up into this gold sun with your arms welcoming it into your space. It fills you up from head to toe, penetrating into the cells of your body and out into your aura.

When you feel filled up, bend forward and shake your shoulders imagining that you are so filled up that there is extra light like glitter falling off you. Sit up with your eyes open and big smile.

Now that you have learned each of the 7 tools, you are ready to perform the "Find Your Space" meditation!

🔊 "Find Your Space" Meditation

(http://www.clairvoyantmeditation.com/book.php)

Close your eyes with a smile and find your clairvoyant center.

Imagine your root chakra in the groin area securely connected to the center of the Earth with a long, hollow grounding cord.

Allow the gravity to gently pull you to the center of the planet and release any tension or uncomfortable feelings such as doubt, uncertainty or resistance down this grounding cord.

Become aware that you are surrounded by a bubble of your own light that is now tightening to an arm's length distance from your body.

This is called your aura and it is your space. Really experience the edge of your "space." See your protection rose in front of you. Notice the beautiful fountains of light moving out the top of your head and hands.

Imagine a golden sun is above your head filling you up with light, amusement, and joy.

Part Three:

Preparation For A Reading
"Energizing Your Reading Screen"

5 Steps to Prepare You for Reading

At this point, you are aware of the abilities in each chakra and can go to your Clairvoyant Center to find your space.

Next, you will go a step further and "read" a person or situation.

Keep in mind that it is essential to be grounded and to Find Your Space before doing a reading. For this reason I list Step #1 simply as "Find Your Space" without any further explanation.

The remaining 4 steps take your through process of what Clairvoyant Practitioners call "energizing your reading screen." Once you have found your space and energized your reading screen, you are fully ready to perform a clairvoyant reading.

Step #1: Find Your Space

Before you conduct any type of reading, it is always best to ground yourself and perform the full "Find Your Space" meditation.

Step #2: Find and Clear Your Reading Screen

Whether you know it or not, you are using your Reading Screen all of the time. With conversations, the news, movies, and your own thoughts, our brains are constantly making associations with symbols and images and creating pictures on a screen in front of our eyes for us to interpret.

On this screen we are reading a combination of body language, physical appearance, as well as the pictures in other people's auras. These pictures we see come from the conversations and thoughts people have. Statements such as "I'm on top of the world today" to " He dumped me" produce pictures for us to see.

Once you become aware of your Reading Screen, you can take charge of the pictures that you see. You can imagine or "create" pictures and then stop seeing them or "clear" the pictures.

You can use your Reading Screen to imagine your

chakras and the energy moving in your body. As you are learning to read and say what you see, you will realize that there is no difference between seeing, knowing, or simply making something up. It all relates to experience in the physical world. As you do these exercises you may see something and then feel like you are simply making it up or just thinking these ideas – but there is no difference – it is all clairvoyance – tuning in and "reading."

 ### *Find Your Reading Screen*

(http://www.clairvoyantmeditation.com/book.php)

 ### *Clear Your Reading Screen*

(http://www.clairvoyantmeditation.com/book.php)

 ### *Ground Your Reading Screen*

(http://www.clairvoyantmeditation.com/book.php)

Sit in a comfortable chair with your feet on the floor. Close your eyes with a smile and briefly touch the center of your forehead to locate your clairvoyant center.

Bring your attention into the room at the center of your head. In this room, imagine yourself sitting down on a comfortable chair or couch that you created and looking through the window that is just above the eyes – in the center of the forehead.

Let this window stretch into the size of a rectangle. You can imagine you are sitting in your own home movie theater.

You can physically locate the reading screen:

Open your eyes and see something in the room. Close them again and continue to see in your mind's eye.

Do this several times, each time seeing more details.

You will notice each time when you close your eyes that you are looking slightly up to an area between the eyes and above the eyebrows.
You can touch this area – it's your sixth chakra.

Clean and Ground Your Reading Screen:
Your reading screen has layers and layers of pictures on it – like clearing bugs on a windshield.

Spray an imaginary solvent on the screen first and

then watch everything melt away.

Take a squeegee and wipe it across the screen clearing it. Like grounding a room, imagine that each corner of the screen is connected into a center grounding cord.

See the screen as clear and clean – anything that enters your thoughts or the screen goes down the grounding cord.

Place a grounding cord on your reading screen so it stays steady and doesn't float. It is clear and takes on the quality of a receptacle for your imagination.

Imagine a rose on the screen with all its petals. Allow yourself to even see dewdrops. Reach out with a big sponge and erase this rose off your screen.

You control what you are looking at – you can create and you
can destroy the pictures on your screen.

It is just as important to erase or destroy what you see on the screen as what you create on the screen. When you take charge of your screen, deciding what you see, you also take charge of your life.

Step #3: Turning Down the Critic

There is a part of your mind called the Critic. This is the part of you that judges and criticizes and doubts all that you see and do. It is difficult to trust what you see unless you turn this down. Postulate that the Critic will remain turned down for the entirety of the reading so you can have fun and certainty while you are saying what you see.

 ***Turning Down the Critic***

(http://www.clairvoyantmeditation.com/book.php)

Sit in a comfortable chair with your feet on the floor. Close your eyes with a smile and briefly touch the center of your forehead to locate your clairvoyant center. See your Reading Screen.

Then, see a circle on your screen. As you look at it, notice that it is becoming a gauge, the kind you'd find on an oxygen tank– with numbers from 0-100 and a small needle that moves and points to the number. Notice the number the needle is pointing to. Imagine you can attach a grounding cord to the gauge.

Listen to the pressure release and see the needle loosen. Use your finger to move the needle to the left, back to 10 on the gauge. See the screen brighten up in the background. With certainty that the Critic will stay at 10 on the gauge, take an eraser in your hand and reach out and erase the circle that you see on the screen. See that the screen is completely clean and clear.

Step #4: Dial Your Chakras

You can think of the chakras in your body as a system of processors – opening and closing in response to your thoughts and the outside world.

Your energy runs through some chakras more than others. In order to perform a clairvoyant reading, you want to send your energy into the upper chakras, particularly the Forehead and Crown. The lower chakras can be turned down so the body feels safe and detached from emotion and responsibility.

You can use your Reading Screen to adjust your chakras.

When you use your Reading Screen, you are in the center of your head, amused and neutral – like watching a movie.

However, unlike a movie, you are not crying or feeling everything with the characters you are watching. You are moving out of the feeling areas by turning those down and turning the observer (your screen) up.

To begin, see and adjust each chakra one at a time on your screen.

When you see a chakra, it looks like a spinning circle with a camera shutter-eye opening and closing on the inside.

You can imagine it resembles a dial.

Dial the Root Chakra

We turn down the root chakra so the body can feel safe and comfortable during the reading. You don't need to be in survival mode.

Dial the Below the Navel Chakra

The Below the Navel chakra contains the abilities of clairsentience and emotions. When you turn this chakra down, you are better able to see rather than feel the person or situation you are reading. Your body is free to not match any of their emotions.

Dial the Stomach Chakra

The Stomach chakra is concerned with power and control. When you turn this down in a reading, you no longer need to give advice or expend effort. If you find yourself feeling effort during the reading or giving advice, check this dial and turn it down. This chakra, also called the Solar Plexus, is an energy source for your body. Thus, it is tuned a bit higher than the other two chakras, so you continue to have energy during the reading.

Dial the Forehead Chakra

The Forehead Chakra is your window and place of clear seeing or clairvoyance. As you turn down the lower chakras, you are able to bring more of your energy and attention to this Forehead Chakra. You can open this chakra up wider, so you can easily see images and colors on your reading screen. The Forehead Chakra is the place for pure observation. With the lower chakras turned down and this one turned up, you can feel free to speak from a place of neutrality, curiosity and amusement.

Set Your Crown Chakra

Your crown chakra located at the top of the head is the place of your own certainty, knowledge, and wisdom. Set your crown chakra not only for a reading but also for any situation where you don't want to match low energy levels or be controlled by the surroundings, such as a dreary, stressful office space or a large stadium or store. Occasionally, check-in with the color of your crown and be amused if it has changed color – simply change it back to the color you chose that makes you amused and neutral.

Recording) Dial Your Chakras

(http://www.clairvoyantmeditation.com/book.php)

Sit in a comfortable chair with your feet on the floor. Close your eyes with a smile and briefly touch the center of your forehead to be present in your clairvoyant center.
Find and Clear your Reading Screen.

See a circle that is spinning on the outside, while opening and closing in the center. This dial represents your Root chakra.

Imagine that you can see a number between 0 and 100 associated with the dial. It can be something you know from your thoughts or a number that actually appears on the dial or next to it. Say the number aloud to affirm that you see the number.

Imagine that a spinning button with numbers pops out the middle and you can use your fingers to turn it down to 10. Allow the dial for your root chakra to close down in size. Just know that it is spinning and adjusting to 10 % open. The energy coming out is brought up to the forehead and top of the head

chakras to enhance the energy there.
See the screen behind the dial getting brighter.

Decide that you are finished looking at the root chakra, take an eraser in your hand and imagine that you are erasing the vision of that chakra off the screen. While keeping your awareness in the center of your head, notice your lower body. Know that your root chakra at the base of your spine has closed down and is spinning with earth and cosmic energies running through. Know also that the grounding cord continues to be firmly connected.

Next, see another dial on the screen – this one represents the Below the Navel chakra. You see it spinning on the outside, while opening and closing in the middle. Imagine that you can see a number between 0 and 100 appear next to this dial. Say the number aloud to affirm what you see and how open this chakra is. No judgment, just remain curious.

Imagine that a spinning button pops out the middle of the dial and you can use your fingers to turn it down to 10. Allow the dial for your Below the Navel chakra to close down in size –just know that it is spinning and adjusting to 10 % open. The energy coming out is brought up to enhance the forehead and top of the head chakras.

Notice the screen behind the chakra getting brighter and brighter. Decide that you are finished looking at the Below the Navel chakra, take an eraser in your hand and imagine that you are erasing the vision of that chakra off the screen. While keeping your awareness in the center of your head, notice your lower body. Know that your Below the Navel chakra has closed down and is spinning freely.

Next, see another dial on the screen – this one is the dial representing the Stomach chakra. You see it spinning on the outside, opening and closing in the middle. Imagine that you can see a number between 0 and 100 appear next to this dial. Say the number aloud to affirm what you see and how open this chakra is. No judgment, just remain curious. Imagine that a button pops out of the middle of the dial and you can use your fingers to turn it down to 30. Allow the dial for your Stomach chakra to adjust in size. Just know that it is spinning and open to 30 %. The energy moving out is brought up to enhance the forehead and top of the head chakras.

Notice the screen behind the chakra getting brighter and brighter. Decide that you are finished looking at the Stomach chakra, take an eraser in your hand and imagine that you are erasing the vision of that chakra off the screen.

While keeping your awareness in the center of your head, notice your stomach area. Know that your Stomach chakra has closed down and is spinning freely.

See the forehead chakra. It is fun to see an eye for this chakra. See the eye containing a beautiful, spinning iris with a pupil that opens and closes in the middle. This chakra has been receiving all the energy moved out of the lower three chakras and is bright and strong (It has 20/20 vision!)

Notice the number associated with this chakra between 0 and 100. Adjust the dial so that it reads 60. Allow the dial for your Forehead chakra to tune to that size. Just know that it is spinning and open to 60%.

Notice the screen getting even brighter. Decide that you are finished looking at the forehead chakra, take an eraser in your hand and imagine that you are erasing the vision of that chakra off the screen.

To do this faster, after you're comfortable with the process, you can imagine a dashboard containing all dials plus the critic guage on the screen. Like a pilot, preparing his instruments in the cockpit, you can adjust the dials quickly. When finished, imagine you can use your eraser to wipe away the whole dashboard at once. Imagine placing a small hat, like a beret, in your favorite color on top of your head. It covers your crown and rests easily there. This color should be one that brings you amusement and joy, offering protection and certainty.

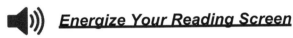

Energize Your Reading Screen

(http://www.clairvoyantmeditation.com/book.php)

Find Your Clairvoyant Center.

Notice all the tools are working. You have your grounding cord, your fountains are running out the top of your head and your hands. You have a protection rose out in front of you pulling your aura around you like an egg.

Find your room in the center of your head. Sit down in your chair and look out at your reading screen. Notice that it brightens and energizes as you hold your attention on it.

To energize it further, you visualize a dashboard with four dials. The dial on the right measures pressure so it looks like a gauge with a needle pointing at a number between "0" and "100."

See the number it is pointing to. Imagine plugging a small grounding cord to this dial and hearing the pressure release. You can now move the needle to "10."

Next see the other dials spinning and opening and

closing. These represent the lower chakras – set them as Root -10, Below the Navel -10, Stomach - 30.

Know that they have closed down and are "set." See the Reading screen as brighter. Bring in a Gold Sun to fill up all the open spaces in your body and aura.

Know that you are ready to do a reading.

Part Four:

Perform a Reading
"The Two Clocks"

Performing A Reading

After you have prepared for the reading by Finding Your Space and Energizing Your Reading Screen, you are ready to perform a reading.

You can read someone in person or from a distance on the phone and tell them what you are seeing. You can also read someone just for your own private curiosity. In this case, you don't have to share what you see, it's for your own information.

What is it like to do a reading?

When we go to the movies we open up our imagination, suspend our disbelief, and lose our sense of time. A reading is much the same way. When you perform a reading, you simply imagine a screen in front of you and look at the pictures (or symbols) that naturally pop up. All of the pictures and symbols have meaning and thus, create a context to interpret what you see.

A reading allows you to tune into someone's innermost desires, life's purpose and relationships that lie just behind the games and drama the person may be experiencing. This communication and new awareness brings healing and positive change to both the reader and the readee. The more you practice readings, the more certainty you gain in accessing your clairvoyant ability in all aspects of your life.

To help you in gaining your clairvoyant certainty, I am now going to teach you a simple and powerful reading technique I call The Two Clocks. In the Two Clocks Reading you will be reading others by first seeing two clocks with two different times on them and then interpreting and explaining the meaning of them.

A Two Clocks reading is part of a broader method of reading called a Symbol Reading. Symbols, in our case 2 clocks, not only represent a deeper part of ourselves, they allow us to suspend our critical voice. When we are just looking for these images, we are no longer thinking with our logical mind but with our creative mind, giving us access to our imagination which is the key to our clairvoyance, creativity and healing powers.

The Two Clocks

This simple reading technique is useful when you just want to know more about someone. This reading can show you how "connected" or aware the person is to their own body.

A person's body and spirit travel separately from each other in time. For example, your spirit, as experienced by your creative thoughts and imagination, can be an hour or more ahead of the body when you are thinking about an event in the future. For example, you can daydream at the beginning of your workday about what you will do when you leave. In this daydream it is already five o'clock pm, so you are eight hours ahead of your body in your imagination and thoughts.

Using the symbols of two clocks, you can see the time difference between the person's body and spirit as well as what is coming between the person's body and spirit. You can see what is pulling their body and spirit closer together (more awareness) and what is pushing their body and spirit apart (distracting them). Often it will be obvious distractions, other times you may be surprised. A person whose spirit is closer to the body is more present and effective in their lives. This reading allows you to see what is distracting this person or keeping them distant as well as what inspires them to come closer to their body.

The Two Clocks reading is simple. The times on the clocks are not significant, just the time difference. Usually a person's spirit is ahead of the body as it tends to travel faster, though sometimes you will find that the person's spirit is behind the body. It is important to remember to open up and let yourself see whatever comes to mind. In the steps, I offer "Tricks to See" to help you open up more and get past the voice of your critic.

Your Spirit and Your Physical Body

To help you understand The Two Clocks even further, here is a deeper explanation of the relationship between your spirit and your physical body...

You have a spiritual body and a physical body. They naturally vibrate at different speeds. The spirit can travel freely with no time or space while the physical body is subject to time and space due to gravity. These two bodies are magnetically held together as long as the physical body is alive. The physical body is only "alive" because of its relationship with the spiritual body.

The closer someone's spirit body is to the physical body, the more awareness and effectiveness they have on the events in their daily life. When the spirit body is vibrating faster or far away, a person may experience "spacey-ness, " and frustration that things are not happening fast enough in their life. Ideally, the spirit and body vibrate close to one another – in terms of time, think of them being an hour apart. In this state, a person experiences inspiration, joy, peace and less effort in their endeavors and relationships as they are more present in their lives.

Through meditation, awareness and intention, anyone can bring the spiritual body closer to the physical body on a more regular basis and even merge the two for short periods of time.

The Two Clocks Reading Technique

Choose someone to read.

You can choose to read anyone since you can do this reading either in person (in the same room or on the phone) or from a distance. If you are reading someone from a distance, this can be private and for your information only.

You don't need to tell the person that you read them. Ideally, you will need the person's first and last name, though the reading can still be done if you only know their first name. You can also read someone just using their picture, if you don't have a name.

When you first begin to practice reading in person, choose people who are willing and open-minded to receiving this kind of spiritual communication. You are building your confidence in using your clairvoyance - the more positive experiences you have, the more certainty you gain. If the person is not open-minded, or you don't know them but are still curious about them, you can read them privately, from a distance.

Here are some ideas for people you can read either

in person or from a distance:

- A person you know well such as a friend or family member.

- A person you don't know well such as an acquaintance, co-worker, future boss, new friend.

- A celebrity or someone you are curious about.

- A person who is far away from you and you want to see how they are doing.

 - A person who is acting differently and you want to know what is going on with them.

- Someone you know as an acquaintance but not real well like a co-worker, boss, interviewer or person you may meet for a date.

- Someone not open to this type of communication; but you just want to know more about them for your own information.

Set Up the Readee.

If the readee is in person, either in the room with you or on the phone, instruct them to:

- Sit across from you (when in the same room), at least an arm's length away, upright in a chair with their legs and arms uncrossed and feet flat on the floor.

- Keep their eyes open during the reading, and

- Line up their chakras with yours.

Important Note: When communicating with the readee, always use clairvoyant words having to do with vision to describe what you see rather than feeling words. This will keep you in your clairvoyant center, neutral and keep the reading from turning into a conversation or a situation in which you need to control what you see about the readee. You are feeling emotions and sensations in your body, but you speak from your visual center.

Use Visual /Clairvoyant words: (upper chakras)

See
Notice
Observe
Visualize

Avoid Sensing/Feeling words: (lower chakras)

Sense
Get
Feel

Avoid Words of Advice:

You need to...
You have to...
It would be better for you to...

For example:

Use "I see that you're restricted by your job" rather than "I feel that you're restricted by your job."

Use "I see you spending more time with your children and experiencing more freedom," rather than "You need to spend more time with your children."

Prepare Yourself for the Reading.

Once the readee is set up, you prepare yourself with a simple "check-in." This is a just a simple review of your tools to know they are working for you:

Find Your Space:
- Close Your Eyes and Touch Your Center
- Smile -- Find Your Amusement
- See Your Grounding Cord
- See the Energy Fountains
- See Your Protection Rose

Energize your Reading Screen:
- Imagine Your Reading Screen in Front of You
- See the Dashboard with 4 Dials:
  Analyzer-10%, 1st Chakra- 10%,
  2nd Chakra- 10%, 3rd Chakra- 30%

Perform the Reading

There are 12 basic steps to The Two Clocks reading:

1. Let the readee know you will be reading them using the symbols of two clocks along with some colors. Let them know you will read the symbols and colors first and then explain what they mean.

2. Have the readee say their full name three times in person or on the phone. If it is a distance reading, you say their name 3 times.

As they say their name, imagine a clock on your screen – it can be digital or old fashioned with hands and numbers or it can just be the thought of a time.

3. Read the time and say it aloud with an "am" or "pm". For example say, "I see the first clock at 12:00 pm."

4. Imagine you can move that clock to the left on your screen and see another clock appear to its right. Read and say the time aloud on that clock with the "am" or "pm."

5. Say the time difference in hours between the clocks.

For example, say "I see the second clock at 4:00pm. I see a 4 hour time difference between the clocks."

6. Look for 2 colors between the clocks.
Say the two colors. If you see three, choose the two colors that are the most bold or interesting. For example: "I see green and purple."

Tricks to See:
Say to yourself "If I could think of or pretend to think of 2 colors what would they be?"

7. Choose and focus on one of the two colors. Trick to See: start with the one that interests you the most. For example: "I am going to look closely at the green color .

8. You will say whatever comes to mind with the following questions (Ask yourself silently):

"As I look at that color, do I notice that color pulling the clocks together or pushing them apart?" (First thought that comes to mind.)

Once you decide, ask yourself:

What qualities, images or ideas are in that color? If nothing comes to mind, you can ask:

"What does that remind me of or make me think about?" (Be curious and open to whatever comes to mind.)
*Be able to feel in your body or think with your imagination (sadness, calm, peace) what part of your own body does it have an effect on?

*Tricks to See:
Say to yourself, "If I could pretend to think of something right now, what would it be?"

Imagine the color as a curtain of that color -- pull it open. What's behind the curtain? Allow yourself to see images, symbols or even a vision of that person acting out something behind it.

Get Curious -- "I wonder what that's about..."

If you see a person, ask yourself if it's a male or a female... then ask yourself if it's a family member or friend or co-worker.

Let Yourself Just Know the answer.

For example, you read the color green first and decide it is pulling the two clocks together. The green reminds you of a beautiful green field and children running. You describe these images to the readee. "I see the color green between the clocks which is pulling them closer together. In this green, I see a green meadow with children running and it makes me think of freedom."

Color #1   (green)
Focus on the second color between the clocks. Say whatever comes to mind with the following questions:

Ask yourself (silently) :
"As I look at that color, do I notice that color pulling the clocks together or pushing them apart?" (First thought that comes to mind)

Once you decide, ask yourself:

What qualities, images or ideas are in that color?

If nothing comes to mind, you can ask:
"What does that remind me of or make me think about?" (Be curious and open to whatever comes to mind.)

Be able to feel in your body or think with your imagination (sadness, calm, peace) what part of your own body does it have an effect on?

*Tricks to See:

Say to yourself, "If I could pretend to think of something right now, what would it be?"

- Imagine the color as a curtain of that color -- pull it open. What's behind the curtain? Allow yourself to see images, symbols or even a vision of that person acting out something behind it.

- Get Curious -- "I wonder what that's about..."

- If you see a person, ask yourself if it's a male or a female... then ask yourself if it's a family member or friend or co-worker.

- Let Yourself Just Know the answer.
For example, you read the second color as purple and decide it is pushing the two clocks apart. You see a purple curtain and pull it away. Behind it, you see the readee sitting at desk in a large room shaped like a box. You see that the box is small and there is a feeling of restriction. You describe these images to the readee. "I see the color purple between the clocks which is pushing them apart. In this purple, I see you sitting a desk with lots of papers in a room. It is cramped and small in the shape of a box. I notice a feeling of restriction.

12. Next, reveal and explain what the symbols and colors mean for the readee. Here's an example of how you can read the meaning of the clocks for the readee:

"The clock on the left represents your Body and the clock on the right represents your Spirit. The colors in between represent what is influencing your relationship between your spirit and body.

I saw that the clock on the left representing your body was at 12:00 pm and the clock on the right representing your spirit was at 4:00 pm. I saw a 4 hour time difference. So your spirit is 4 hours ahead of your body. With this time difference, I see that you may be experiencing some frustration at getting things you want quickly. The green color I saw is pulling your spirit and body closer together- this shows me the ideas of freedom, nature and children. From this, I see you are enjoying your time with nature and children and this heals you. The other color which was purple is pushing your body and spirit apart and I notice it is making you feel stressed and distant. I also notice that you are restricted by your job and not able to experience the freedom you are seeking."

End the Reading

It is important to have the readee replenish their energy after a reading. It is a healing process to receive communication about themselves. In this process, they release energy and open themselves up to bring in more of their own energy. It is also important for the readee to know that the reading is ending so they don't continue to ask you questions informally about it later. This is a formal reading with a beginning and an end.

Bring in a Golden Sun

Ask the Readee to imagine a Golden Sun filling them up from the crown of their head all the way through to their feet.

For example: "Please close your eyes and imagine a golden sun over your head. This is made of your own highest creative life force energy coming back to you from all the people, places and events from the past, present and future. This sun is filled with joy, inspiration and peace. Reach your arms up into it and allow it to fill up all the open spaces that were created during this reading today along with all the cells of your body from head to toe."

Make Separations

Have the readee imagine a book with their name and today's date on the cover. Tell them to see the last page with the words "The End." Have them close the book and blow it up.

For example: "Please imagine an important book out in front of you. The title on the cover is "Your Reading" with your name and today's date. We will turn to the last page of the book and see the words 'The End.' We will close the book and blow it up. Now the reading has ended and we are each on our own separate paths."

Replenish Yourself

Use an eraser to clear your screen and bring in your own Golden Sun.

Even if this is a distance reading, be sure to fill up with a Golden Sun and make separations by closing the book for yourself.

 ***Two Clocks Reading***

(http://www.clairvoyantmeditation.com/book.php)

Summary

There Is A Voice Inside Of You
That Whispers All Day Long,
"I Feel That This Is Right For Me,
I Know That This Is Wrong."
No Teacher, Preacher, Parent, Friend
Or Wise Man Can Decide What's Right For You-
Just Listen To The Voice That Speaks Inside.

— Shel Silverstein

Shel Silverstein was a champion for the encouraging and playful voice inside of all of us. Through riddles, poems and silly drawings, he opened up people's amusement and imagination with clever truths that challenged readers to expand their minds. Through simple, yet profound, themes and images, Silverstein appealed to our creative, inner voice rather than the critical one.

In this same way, a clairvoyant reading opens up the inner voice. When you practice using your clairvoyant tools, you not only gain a new way of thinking and seeing the world, but you also gain certainty in listening to your inner voice.

With practice, you no longer doubt your own ideas allowing this inner voice to become the dominant voice rather than the critical one. You give yourself permission to see and know things for yourself and to speak your truth to yourself and to others that heals and brings light in the world. You realize that have a network of extra- senses that are operating for you and, when you learn to control them and work with them, you can take charge of your life.

Having a clairvoyant perspective allows you to see the truth of any situation and stay neutral and amused. It also allows you to heal others just through your words. Rather than agreeing with someone's problem or giving advice, you communicate a vision of them as more whole and healed. ("I see you eating healthy food and feeling better.")

You move out of the sympathetic space of seeing them as a victim. Instead you become a witness to them as a capable spirit going through a special process of growth. The other person is free to see this vision with you and release their emotions without worrying about your feelings.

You let go of limiting beliefs. Often, when you are looking at beliefs and situations that create limits in someone else's life, you realize you have matching concepts in your own life. As you communicate to the person, you can see these limits and beliefs more clearly in your own life and use your clairvoyant tools to move past them with neutrality and amusement.

All along, you are gaining certainty that you can use clairvoyance in your own life.

Appendix #1:

Examples of "Two Clocks" Readings

Examples of "Two Clocks" Readings

Here are some examples of real readings I have performed using the Two Clocks Technique. I have included the readee's feedback as well.

****

Example Reading #1:

I am going to read the time on two clocks with colors in between. I will first read what I see, then explain what they mean. I see the first clock, on the left, at 1pm and the second clock, on the right, at 5 pm. There is a four hour time difference between the two clocks.

I see the colors orange and green between the clocks. The orange color is pushing the clocks apart, while I see the green pulling the clocks together.

The orange has the quality and feeling of discomfort and I see a symbol of a hand with red fingers. The green has the quality and feeling of laughter and nature. I see the image of 2 deer running in a field - a large one and a baby. The baby has spots on it and it's following its mother closely.

The clock on the left represents your body and the clock on the right represents your spirit. I see that your spirit is four hours ahead of your body. The closer your spirit is to your body, the more grounded you feel in your relationships and projects and the quicker you manifest what you want in your life.

The orange that represents what is pulling your spirit away from the body has the quality of discomfort and specifically in your hands or fingers. It looks like a physical ailment in that area. The hands represent creativity and healing as well as the direction in which a lot of your attention is going.

You are healing people in your life through your hands or creative projects and this takes you away from healing yourself. The second color, green, represents what is helping you get closer to your body or healing your spirit and body relationship. There is laughter and nature in this color. The deer represent the innocence and sweetness of nature and the mother child bond.

I see that you enjoy being in nature and these experiences bring you closer to your body and a healing from all the stress of healing others.

Readee's feedback:

She revealed that she is a dentist and is literally uses her hands to heal other people. She has also had stiffness in her fingers lately and has been taking aspirin to relieve the symptoms. She has been dreading the longer procedures as her hands begin to ache. Her patients have also become more demanding. Thus, she has been thinking about cutting back her schedule. The deer represent the actual deer she has been seeing in her backyard in New Jersey. She lives on a large, open property and there is a family of deer that has been greeting her every morning as she looks out her kitchen window. She has been looking forward to seeing them and having powerful moments watching the mother and baby. (The readee had tears in her eyes at the fact the deer came through the reading to say "hello.") She realizes that nature is healing her. She also recognized that her own intuition has been telling her to cut back on her patient load so she can heal physically and spiritually.

Example Reading #2:

I am going to read the time on two clocks with colors in between. I will first read what I see, then explain what they mean. I see the first clock, on the left, at 10:00 pm and the second clock, on the right, at

130

2:00 pm -- the same day. There is an eight hour time difference between the two clocks with the clock on the right behind the clock on the left.

I see the colors red and brown between the clocks. The red color is pushing the clocks apart, while I see the brown pulling the clocks together. The red has the quality of passion and excitement and I see a pointed mountain with fire or actually, a volcano. The brown has the quality and feeling of family and comfort. In this color, I see the image of an older woman and another image of a house.

The clock on the left represents your body and the clock on the right represents your spirit. I see that your spirit is eight hours behind your body. The closer your spirit is to your body, the more grounded you feel in your relationships and projects and the quicker you manifest what you want in your life.

It is unusual to have your spirit behind your body so I will also look to see what is happening here. I see that the red is really pulling your spirit away from your body with its feeling of excitement. The volcano is a symbol of something exploding or changing greatly in your life. This looks like a move or a significant change in your living situation.

It looks like the fact that your spirit is going behind

your body is because of this volcano - the move itself is drawing you this direction. Your spirit and body are separated by eight hours and this makes it hard to focus or concentrate on regular tasks. I see that the brown is comfort and home. The woman looks like your mother. Your mother and the comfort of your home are healing you and grounding you during this big change in your life.

Readee Response:

She revealed that she and her family will be moving to Hawaii from the East Coast in a couple of months. The house they were moving into is at the base of a volcano. She has to sell her house and leave her mother and father behind on the mainland in California.

She was amused because Hawaii is exactly eight hours behind the East Coast and she has had her thoughts and energy on her future home. Her mother has offered to pack up things for her and help with the move.

She was considering letting her mother help in this way. The sale of the house would create money to help her feel more secure about the expenses of the move. She had just heard they had a buyer and the home sale was close to coming through.

This reading helped her make sense of her anxiety and made her realize she had to be more present and bring her thoughts and awareness into her current home and time zone until she was leaving.

She realized excitement and anticipation are wonderful, but they are ungrounded emotions which bring anxiety. She decided to gain control over this so she can get everything done and enjoy herself more. She also decided to let her mother help more with the move.

Example Reading #3:

(Long Distance Reading for personal information done by a student in my clairvoyant class)

Situation: There is a man I am working with who always seems distracted and not interested in my projects. What is going on with him?

Spoken to self:

I see the first clock, on the left, at 2 pm and the second clock, on the right, at 2 am the next morning. There is a twelve hour time difference between the two clocks. I see the colors silver and white between the clocks. The silver color is pushing the clocks apart, while I see the white pulling the clocks together.

The silver has the quality and feeling of magic, laughter and love and I see a symbol of a star. In fact, I see lots of stars. The white has the quality and feeling of clouds -- no real feelings just numbness. I see the image of clouds as if I'm looking out an airplane window.

I also see that there is a red color behind the white cloud material. This has the quality of tension and stress. I see the images of computers, desks and offices in this color.

The clock on the left represents his body and the clock on the right represents his spirit. I see that his spirit is twelve hours ahead of his body. I know that the closer his spirit is to his body, the more grounded he feels in his relationships and projects and the quicker he can manifest what he wants in his life.

He can also take more interest in my projects if he is closer to his body. From this, I see that this man is distant and distracted. He is out of his body by 12 hours. It is interesting that the silver is so positive and it's pulling his spirit away from the body. It looks like he prefers to be out of his body.

The red that pulls him into his body looks like his work and the white clouds look like unconscious thoughts and daydreams around this work. This white also looks like resistance to the work. This man does not look fulfilled by this work - rather wants to be in this place with stars and prefers to go there and be out of his body. I see that he is distracted by the need to escape work and that his lack of interest in my projects has nothing to do with me.

Reader's Revelations:

Shortly after doing this reading, I traveled to his house for a company dinner party. There were star stickers all over the front windows. I learned at the party that his three young children had decorated the windows. I realized that the stars in the reading represented the children he so longed to spend more time with. I didn't realize he had three young children. The twelve hour difference in the clocks represented the number of hours he was sometimes away from them on his business trips.

This reading gave me more insight and compassion

for my co-worker. I realized sometimes people force themselves to do things they don't want to do. This makes them more distant and thus ineffective in their work and relationships. I saw that I did this as well and decided to stop resisting my choices for work and places and to be more present and appreciative in my own life.

Appendix #2:

Miracle Stories

Miracle Stories

At the beginning of each class, my students share stories that reflect how their new clairvoyant tools are affecting their lives. We call them "miracle stories." Students enjoy these stories because they feel they are part of a magical community. They also gain ideas from others about how the tools can be used in their daily lives. By sharing these stories here, I hope to achieve the same for you. The following are true stories told by my clairvoyant students:

****

I am a nurse at a hospital emergency room. I decided to use the grounding cord tool to calm the chaos of my workplace. As in any emergency room, I always experienced feelings of fear and panic along with disorganization. Before work, I sat in my car in the hospital parking lot and imagined the building surrounded in gold and connected to the center of the earth by a large grounding cord. I then visualized the words "Everything's okay" above each person's head. When I went in to the hospital that day, I noticed an extreme difference - there was laughter and calm where before there had been fear, complaining and anxiety. I also felt energized at the end of my ten hour shift rather than exhausted. This was a true miracle.

****

*When I started to feel overwhelmed by the stuffy &
crowded bar room at my friends' engagement party, I
went to the bathroom to get space and use my tools. First,
I grounded myself and the whole restaurant. Then I
imagined gold suns pouring through the place to lighten
and brighten the place. Upon returning from the
bathroom a few minutes later, half the party had left and
a giant window had been opened (in the middle of winter
no less).*

****

*I was at the gym this morning, in a hot, stuffy spin room.
I decided to ground the room and fill it with bright, white
light. I could hear you saying that nothing can hide from
the light. A few minutes later, the instructor made an
announcement that something odd was going on because
no one's heart monitor was working. She said "this is so
weird!" I think the white light altered the
electromagnetic frequency of the room. Now I know this
really works!*

****

I used my protection rose for a phone call. My sister-in-law likes to call and complain about her life several times a week. I usually listen and give her advice and feel upset by the end of the call. This time when the phone rang and I saw it was her, I first imagined my protection rose in front of me and then picked up the phone. As she was speaking, I imagined the rose in front of me. I allowed all her words to go into the rose. I was able to stay relaxed, amused and neutral during the conversation. I just let her know I was listening and found it easy to not give advice. I just let her release into my rose. When the phone call was over, I blew up the rose and felt great!

****

I am a medical office manager and work with people of various personalities. One woman whose desk was next to mine was always complaining to the other office workers and sour with the patients. I knew that if this continued, I would have to fire her. In order to avoid this confrontation, I decided to use my new clairvoyant tools. Each time I meditated, (grounded, ran my energy and filled myself with gold suns) I imagined that she was smiling at me. I pictured her letting go of the complaints down her own grounding cord. I imagined that she had her own gold suns to fill herself up. I saw her filled with gold light. As I imagined this for her, I saw her smiling and acting friendly. A few days later, she began to confide to me that she has been afraid that her mother was aging and would soon need extra care. She apologized for being unfriendly and told me how much she appreciated working with me! Now she's an easy person to work with and she's become a friend! I didn't have to do anything directly -- just visualize the tools for someone and see them at their best. What a miracle!

****

I just got hired at my first job as a professional psychologist at a homeless shelter in the Bronx. Along with the grounding cord for the building and neighborhood and my protection rose to contain my aura, I wanted to find a quick way to communicate with my new co-workers and patients. I decided to use the tool of setting my crown chakra. I placed an imaginary, bright gold hat on my head that felt like amusement and certainty. This color conveyed that "I knew what I was doing," even though I was brand new and nervous. As I met with co-workers and patients, I held that color in my crown chakra by visualizing my gold hat. Throughout the day people mentioned that I seemed like I've been there longer than just one day. I was also able to stay present in my conversations and even found myself relaxed, smiling and laughing on a day that should have been nerve-racking . Patients and my co-workers were easy to work with and the first day went smoothly. This was a true miracle.

****

As a new clairvoyant student, I had been practicing and playing with the grounding cord tool. I learned that I could not only ground myself to feel more clear and organized, but I could ground objects to keep them more connected to me. I had been grounding my favorite black leather purse as practice. I visualized a strong cord from the purse into the ground and a connection to my below the navel chakra --after all, the purse had my money in it! One day, at a picnic in a large park, I had to carry many things from the car and left my purse on the front seat. My car was in view of the picnic area and when I dropped my things off, I looked back at my car and saw a man opening the car door and reaching for my black purse! He quickly shut the door with my purse in his hand and began walking down the street! I instantly remembered the grounding cord that I had given it and made it stronger -- I imagined the cord pulling the purse to the ground and attached to my below the navel chakra firmly. Just before I yelled "Hey! That's mine!" the purse dropped out of his hand and rolled down the sidewalk towards me. The man looked shocked and ran away. All my valuables are grounded to the earth and to my body now - including my children and pets.

****

To find out more about Tori's upcoming
lectures, appearances, and workshops,
or to get a personalized clairvoyant reading
from Tori (either by Skype, e-mail, or in-person) please visit us at:

http://www.ClairvoyantMeditation.com

http://www.UpayaHouse.com

or Call:

1-800-528-4191

Made in the USA
Charleston, SC
12 November 2013